For Dan,
In honor of
Walker Stevens

Bernie

our daily words

Bernard Horn

D0124915

Old Seventy Creek Press 2009 Poetry Series Prize Award

For my wife, Linda,
and for my daughters,
Gabriella, Hedya, and Rebecca

acknowledgements

"So There It Is," *Moment Magazine*
"On Plum Island," *Dark Horse*
"Our Daily Words," *The Mississippi Review*
"Two or Three Things," *The Huffington Post*

I would also acknowledge my family, my friends, and the writers, notably, Alan Feldman, who have read or heard my poems for many years and confirmed my sense of myself as poet.

All illustrations by Linda Klein
Cover: *Lost Time* (intaglio)
Interior illustrations: from a series of gouaches, *Talitot Nof* ("Landscape Prayer Shawls"), painted in Israel at the same time that many of the poems in Part Four were written.

Book design by Claire Taylor Hansen

OLD SEVENTY CREEK PRESS POETRY SERIES 2010

2010 OLD SEVENTY CREEK FIRST EDITION
PRINTED IN THE UNITED STATES OF AMERICA

PUBLISHED IN THE UNITED STATES
BY OLD SEVENTY CREEK PRESS
RUDY THOMAS, PUBLISHER
P. O. BOX 204
ALBANY, KENTUCKY 42602

ISBN: 1450526004
EAN: 9781450526005

PRINTED BY CREATE SPACE FOR
OLD SEVENTY CREEK PRESS

contents

three: paint her 45

four: two or three things 57

one:

the smell of time

The Smell of Time

Again a large late fall rain
splashes into sodden leaves,
my mouth dries up, and a drier
chill catches my chest, no warmer
than if I were outside, a soaked
long sleeved blue shirt
sticking to my skin, *helpless, help-*
less, Neil Young's voice rings in my mind as I cross
to the mantle and fill my left hand
with the off-white jade turtle
carried to me two years ago from Mexico
by a woman who never again

. . . . In a rush my flesh
fills, as the warmth and almost softness
of the roughly carved idol
floods the secret conduits from fingers and palm,
and I remember other smaller rains and narrow droughts:
my detachment, age eight, from my first death
after I discovered a dried up turtle
in its gallon globe; my delight
years later when I learned
that the whole world rests
on the back of a turtle.
The wind rises, raindrops smack against
the pane, and suddenly my fingertips
are penetrating the softness
beneath the yellow sectioned belly armor of the dead turtle,
and I can't remember the beast's name,
its sex, that I forgot to water its home,
or even what I was feeling, only the smell,

which fills my nostrils, clenches my throat,
presses the tops of my lungs, trying like hell
not to admit
the smell of death, yes,

time enters the mind on waves of odor:
in chills and songs, in turtle eyes
that are sharp black dots
on warm jade, in the tastes
we remember, we relive
and get recaptured by our old attachments,

but the smell of time
pushes us out of our minds
into a stiff wind
that slices through
and cuts us off,
that now, dry,
shakes and flicks the few dangling droplets
from the tips of the branches
and the edges
of the last four yellow leaves
and stirs along the ground
the glistening
brown and leafy mass
decaying to loam, rustling,
rising up, settling,

a wind that moans
and whistles—a quick cold breath
through clenched teeth—as it squeezes
its fresh and chilling way
through the blistered wooden panes
that kept today's downpour
off my back.

The Tel

As fine ice pellets sting the bedroom windowpanes,
my desert sunrise blaze of a dream—
the wind-smoothed mound of sand
containing the residue
of five thousand years of living—
dissolves to the rounds
of cheeks and chin, your face
in predawn light, this time
not your eyes,
but the dark hollow below your lower lip,
and your neck poised, just so,
dissolving gravity, it beckons
for lips, light tongue, cool breath,
for fingertips to trace the shifts of terrain upward—
the soft flesh below the ear, the line
of the jaw, the transformation of driftwood, the miraculous
erosion—the wind, the rain—of mesas, the sharp lines
of sandcastles sculpted, smoothed, mellowed
by receding waves so that one surface flows into
another, and it is clear
that the site in the desert lived along the coast
when some ancient seaport flourished there,
that sandstone walls, gold towers, and the dark green sea
dazzled under desert summer sky and sun,
that the sands
moved slowly as millennia came
and went until the coast grew away
from the walls, wharves, houses, the well kept stone streets,
now at the center of a mound a hundred miles from water,
and that the voices and footfalls of merchant seamen
and poets haunt the buried streets where once they breathed
the warm salt air you would breathe
now.

A Walk

Of course you didn't
—after we'd collided, shared an elate moment
for the first time in six weeks—
walk with me to the Charles and sit there,

your thigh grazing mine, our four feet dangling
from the high weathered splintery bench
a few yards from the brown water that was
rippling, grabbing brilliant patches of sunlight
from the yellow white glare an hour above the stadium

as the choric hum of rush hour cars rose from Storrow Drive
and bundled coxswains shouted lightly dressed oarsmen
home, and one single scull, then a second,
slipped downstream.

It was one walk we'd never taken. An old bench
we'd never shared. And never would. The thing is
when I returned to my room and the pillow you'd sewn
months ago and the stereo I still haven't bought, it seemed
I had walked alone for the very first time
along a path we had always shared.

On Plum Island

What was it that drew my eyes
so to the white bird across the marshes
on Plum Island last August I could have stared

for hours. The kids
after tugging and scrambling for their turns
at the binoculars impatient immediately
for the beach, unlike
your friend's husband the-American-tourist-abroad he was
done (it could have been a kingfisher! a phoenix!)
he handled our attraction
with a fancy telephoto 35 millimeter photograph in the
mist and I
could have stared for days could have

have watched have been a bird
watcher a bird watcher! I
Brooklyn born raised in Manhattan
knowing only the murmurs and droppings
the flights of flocks to roofs
of pigeons how to trap them under fruit crates
hand feed them in the park I could have stared

white and tall
swan neck awkward on spindle legs
poking around the marsh plants through occasional blurs
of ground fog, ducking his head, strolling,
undistracted by birdwatchers
his image magnified
by the lens
beyond my grasp
as he wanders
foraging, his elegance
careless and absolute.

The Shape of Things, July, 1976

Not work, not sweet wine, not cocaine: when my
attention rests equally on the contour
of a stainless steel teaspoon, the purple
residue of blueberry yogurt along the edge, at the bottom
of a paper cup, and my anger
that the woman I love does
what I don't want her to do,

an anger, I realize,
that lacks the stain of condemnation that would make it righteous,

just then does my soul
cry out in solidarity and community
with Dora Bloch, aged, infirm, torn
from her hospital bed by Ugandan thugs,
as the strains of We Shall Overcome
call all of us together under father King's peaceful blessing
as Coretta and Carter face each other
in seemly colloquy, and ladles that dipped
cool rain water from wooden barrels pass forever
from black hands to white hands, white hands
to black hands, dozens of human lips
sipping carefully, uncontrollably trembling
for the lions of Munich, Uganda,
and Mississippi

> *You are lucky to be travelling with me,*
> said Pasco Cohen at Entebbe Airport.
> *I'm a specialist in getting out of the most dangerous*
> *places. I was one of the few survivors*
> *of the Holocaust. I've taken part in all*
> *of Israel's wars and I've faced death many times.*

This time, of course, death had it
its way: he died of loss of blood, with
Ida Borowicz,
Jean-Jacques Maimoni,
Yehonatan Netanyahu. God gives. God takes.
Let freedom ring (softly)

and justice. So that my soul need mobilize
itself and its tears no longer
for one more imperfect victim, one more act
of grandeur or magnanimity.

Let freedom ring

and peace. So that my soul can seek eternity
in how my father's anger lives in mine
and in the shapes of spoons, lives,
and purple stains on waxy white surfaces.

Did You Know

Did you know—
            forsythia's named for
                        William Forsyth (1737–1804)?
            It grows in Gamache's back yard
near the bottom of the dirt road
            that separates your house
                        from John and Eve's—
We could pick the not quite flowering branches
            on the way home
                        shoes wet
            from our first walk on Wangumbaug Lake,
the top of the thick ice pack
            coated now
                        with an airy thinness of slush—
Are you afraid
            now? Are you also remembering
                        the day before yesterday
            when the crack! of the thaw
at three in the morning
            smacked us wide awake
                        hearts racing into spring?
Let's go. The frayed bottoms of our blue jeans
            will be stained black
                        from the rich mud in the woods
            near the limestone cliffs
where some snow has still not melted
            and you can smell
                        last autumn
            in the dank and breathing
dirt.

two:

our daily words

Late Afternoon: A Phone Call

Engaged to someone else, I hear one part
of a conversation between a woman
I had loved and the man she didn't marry.
Dry words squeeze from her throat. As he summons

intimacy, she shares intimacies—
"hard words with my father Sunday morning"—
to keep the conversation going, leery
words cluttering every pause, careening

between familiar proper nouns: Lesley,
El Paso, her fist clenched white, her visage gray,
her jaw moving nonstop beneath her fleshy
cheeks and lips, she jams words into every
silence to keep the man she didn't marry
from filling them up with what he does not say.

The Spirit of Place

In the din of my gifts—a book of photos
by Gordon Parks, a Care Bear, a doll's house
roll top desk and bathtub, one elegant
brown suede shoe—I had forgotten what you'd
given me: besides everything else—the slow
twelve hour drive through Colorado skies; love
on a hillside overlooking a wide valley,
a miracle of many shining greens
to have been held in perpetual possession by the Utes
as long as the sun shines and grass grows green;
a feast in the best place in Colorado
Springs, where we danced to a one-man reggae
band, II moving with grace enough for discrete
gray-haired glances and one couple to think us
"professionals" and a large man, hand
on my arm, to ask, "Are you Islanders?"—

you also gave me your favorite painting,
the corner of your bedroom in Israel:
the narrow window in the middle overlooks
some old red roofed houses, trees, a blue truck
as wide as my thumb, a distant sand hill
rising to meet the pale blue sky. On the top
shelf of a tan cupboard, a well-wrought vase,
a bowl of fruit, and a shadowed bottle
glow in the dazzle of the bright clear day.
Below the shelf the cupboard has just
swung open to the darkness within,
and floating along the boundary between
inside and outside, translucent white robes
of three ghostly figures—parents? a child?—
huddle together against the ultra-
marine blue of the walls and bind the cupboard,
the room, the long view from the window, you,
your dead father, your mother, and your daughters,
your land, your life, and your work: hovering,
they weave it all together and to me.

Catherine Cover Watson

Bright September Sunday morning breakfast,
three weeks married, I've just removed wax seals
from jars of home-made jam, one peach, one plum,
and I think they're your mother's like the others,
but you say, no, they're your sister Dian's,
and your mother's jams always turned out too
gluey or too sweet, and that never stopped her.
And I: "Her mother must have loved her," taking
up our earlier talk that no man who's been
his mother's favorite knows what it is
to fear failure, and your mother made you,
Judie, Lucretia, Dian, whomever
she was with at the time, feel:
"She loves me best."

And though you will defend cold Grandmother Cover—
"she-always-gave-us-ginger-snaps"—her still
politeness, her devotion to violets
and an immaculate home,
                              you preferred
her "devoted" husband, your favorite, who'd
sworn off drink and a wild life after taking
a tumble down the attic stairs in his
Santa Claus get-up and breaking bones,
who, every morning forced insulin into
his thigh, while she, every morning, dressed
her leg wound,
                    and you will recall Dian's version
that Grandma's wound was milk leg that festered
after the birth of your mother, Catherine,
and her twin, Sylvester, the only children,—

now all you get out is
what you will soon explain is your mother's
version from when you were ten or eleven,
that Grandma Cover was scratched by the cat

and never left home again, and your whole
body jerks and shudders, sobs and tears burst
all over the place, and five months have passed
and no time has passed since your mother died.

Our Daily Words

*Who can concentrate on thoughts of scripture or
philosophy and be able to endure babies crying, nurses
soothing them with lullabies, and all the noisy coming
and going of men and women about the house?*
—Peter Abelard, *Historia calamitatum*

The old familiar talk, that
everything passes, that nothing
passes or is certain, that language
itself only yearns, can never inhabit
this earth that recedes from articulation
like a calf forever just eluding
the red hot iron, the insistent
talk, last night, of Chekhov's words and life
rang true, and yet, snowed in
in Framingham, a Tuesday workday,
schoolday, Hedya and I
tramping, sculpting, repeatedly
sledding a long run in the thick snow
on thin plastic sheets, one red,
one blue, while Gabi and you
prepare the first full lunch
we've all sat down to together in longer
than any of us remembers:
Hebrew National salami on rye,
Campbell's salt-and-wonton soup,
cucumbers, scallions, hot spiced cider, words
knocking against words, and Hedya dancing to
Isn't She Lovely in her long johns,
aching for her seventh birthday, so filled
with pleasure, she calls her pal, Prageeta,
and bursts into laughter before she finishes
dialing, while Gabi, darkly gorgeous today,
alternately three years older and younger
than twelve, suddenly, formally,
rises, walks around the table,

plants a kiss on your cheek,
walks back to her chair, sits,
shoots a grin at me, and now,
from her bedroom, yells
for the spelling of "science" but presses
against my left side at this desk before
I get to the "i," while Hedya leans in,
hangs around my other side, writing, "aske,"
"dabe," "eat," "fed," on labels for me to read
out loud before she sticks them
to the back of my sweater, while you're
on the phone with Bev, and then,
lunchtime, and now, at my desk, and now, and
now, I'm almost crying, thinking of
Max von Sydow with the juggler's family
in the clearing eating wild strawberries.
Holding in two long hands a large wooden bowl of milk,
he stares at everything and says unnecessarily
that he will carry the memory of that moment
between his hands
as if it were a wooden
bowl filled to the brim
with fresh milk.

To Comfort the Heart's Core Against Its Small Disasters

Although the part of me that deflects the evil eyes
that slide across Rebecca's face at Purity Supreme
bridles against setting these words down
or saying them out loud, I know:
Nothing in her power will earn Hedya
the love her father feels for Gabi, forever
four years older, and her pain will be
perpetual. As for me, Stepfather, I find myself
listing her accomplishments when her father
shows up every other week,
as if to make him see her as I do, as if,
by my intervention, the pain
could be anything but perpetual.

When Gabi returns Sunday morning
from two days alone with her father
to pick up her books for Hebrew school,
she pauses in the doorway of our bedroom,
sees Rebecca—all four months of her—
Hedya, you, and me cuddled under the covers,
and edges to the foot of the bed, she,
beautiful and neat in her purples and ribbon barrettes,
we tangled, in the chaos and warmth
of bedclothes, near sleep: Does she yearn
to join us? Does she feel a pang like mine
when we moved Rebecca
from the white wicker basket in our bedroom
to the brown crib in her sisters' room? Does she feel
she will never be part of that ensemble
Hedya plays in so easily? Or does she
like looking on, is she pleased by her distance
as she sprints towards puberty, that familiar
distance so like her father's?
Is her pain, too, perpetual?

We would draw her to us, draw her
in. I would tell her . . . But she's twelve,
looking ten, now, at the foot of the bed.
I say, "She was up too late
last night at the party,"
when she says, "Isn't Hedya coming?"
A faint honk. She's gone. As for me,
have I only imagined the plea in her voice?—
"Isn't Hedya coming?"
Desolate. My soul's too slow. An instant
I could have seized, pain I could have diminished
right here, right now, early on,
an instant in the world's life, in Gabi's memory,
has slipped through my fingers. I don't shout, "Stay!"
The outside door closes.
I don't race from the bed. I listen
and roll back to my nest.

Later she will tell you
that she knows her father's jealous of me,
that she loves her father's lover no less than me,
and as I write, now, she wants
her kiss goodnight and I'm
furious! I dream of uninterrupted moods
that swell or splash with no distraction
as I also dream of making it
on the distractions. On the edge of her bed
a minute later, she's telling me
she never wants us to leave at night,
and I know she means her room
not the house, and she pulls
my left arm under her head
and asks me to tickle her neck
"for just a little while."
And as I say these words,
the healing touch of the web of my life
comes over me again, while my mind burns.

I know, or ought to, that I will never
be Father, Daddy, to Gabi, that a single word
that intimates disapproval demonstrates again
that I don't love her at all, that I will never
be the parent yearned for, and the other night
I was making fettuccini Bernardo
with Jarlsburg, mozzarella, parmesan, and havarti,
and the salad she loves, of olive oil, pepper, lemon, and salt
on finely chopped cucumber, parsley, scallion, tomato,
and she said she was too young at the time
to understand the divorce and "maybe
that was easier." "And maybe harder, too,"
I said. "You couldn't say what you meant."
I told her how Gene Hackman in *Night Moves*
tells his wife how he traced his father
who'd abandoned him many years before
to a bench in a small park, how he watched the old man
sitting for awhile, didn't approach or say
a word, and left. Gabi listened, all eyes,
took a deep breath, and another,
and sang a high note,
holding it until I joined
our call and response, high notes and low notes,
me off-key, she at the center of each note,
then long notes, then longer notes, and longer,
as I mixed the melted cheeses into the fettuccini.

The next day I drop what I'm doing,
help her with her French, and tell her not to call her mother a
jerk, even "kidding." Later, in the keen
of her twelve-year-old voice rising from her room,
I hear the wives of Irish fishermen on the cold shore
after a killer storm, huddled, each folded inward
in a dark cloak on the gray wharf. I head for her room
to help with the consolation, fool that I am:

Nailed in her doorway,
I am her culprit. She knows, you tell me later,
she hates me most when I help her, as if
to let me help her is to love me as she loves
her father. She amazes me. I seethe for a breath.
Then resentment gives way to pain gives way to
wonder: "She knows!"
What will be her sea of memories
ten years from now and twenty?
What will be her story of these years?

At eight she traded her daddy, her place,
her sense of friendship, her language,
and finally her mommy for these
United States and me, and all the things
she throws into her hollow maw reverberate,
a drum skin around an emptiness—
will her heart be filled and her soul less hungry?
Will fettuccini and Israeli salad echo in her memory
the way the gray-boned skeleton
of the museum's tyrannosaurus miles
above my head and my chubby arms wrapped tight
around my father's leg rattle around in my mind
seven years after his mind was shattered?

Or we're acting silly and working on her math before bed,
and then she can't see a friend after school tomorrow
because we need an hour's babysitting,
and she throws me a glare of hatred
as if I'd just cut down her daddy and stolen her mommy,
and the old agony twists,
scrapes, and slowly diminishes:
I'm not thinking, "I'm so nice,
she'd better be grateful or else," no,
I'm just here, wide open, again furious
I must be alert to the hatred,
astonished, too, that she knows

she hates me when I'm kind;
I want the rage her hatred triggers to strike
less sharply, but I must protect myself, too,
from this child's fierceness—
better to move in slow motion
for a time and let the sadness
breathe awhile, flame
up, flourish, and
subside, and only then
watch the hotter anger rise up
to put out the other blaze. I must
be with her and
watch myself with her
at the times I would give anything
not to be watching.

So when she let it slip out, a couple of months later
that she sort of had her first boyfriend,
I felt the ogre-daddy rise in me:
how we laughed when we saw the cute
curly-haired red head who could pass for ten,
not the young Hell's Angel of my fantasy,
looming on the stage of the middle school auditorium,
and I knew she would never love me
according to my bond and that all
of our pain could be perpetual

like mine, half-aware, the day before yesterday
when she spent the whole afternoon poring over
packets and packets of photos, slowly assembling
a collage of her pictures, her father
in many, Hedya, you, and Rebecca in a few.
After a quick twinge for myself (I will never
be the parent longed for) I thought of my
father, gone from me this autumn
seven years after the stroke
had deadened his right side,

turned his powerful right hand into a thick shiny claw, and
shattered his language, and my mind swung back to Gabi
and the sixty years of life and more before her,
and I thought of her remembering
and how remembrance dissolves and redeems,
and I saw that she could just as soon
keep the love I feel for her out, keep it out
until she is forty or fifty, but if she lets it in then,
oh, if she lets it in then.

My Father, the Swimmer

Summer, 1952

I don't remember clearly the coming or the going,
the short walk at your side from the rented room or bungalow
to the beach and back, my hand lost in yours, my legs
scurrying to keep up. What does stay in my mind is sitting
on the top pipe railing on the boardwalk at Rockaway
Beach, the silver-painted zinc of the pipe always damp in
the salty ocean air and slightly rough. I'm eight or nine, and
it's easy to conjure the two of us up in the eight o'clock
light of a hot August evening. You've just arrived after
a ten-hour day in your narrow housewares and toy store on
Avenue D; whenever I entered the store as a kid, I always
felt I was entering the bottom of a chasm and the shelves in
the walls were nooks and crannies containing anything anyone
could imagine, somewhere between the floor and the high,
high ceiling. I remember how you used to leap upwards,
precariously balanced at the edges of the shelves as you rose
to retrieve some object, a Monopoly game or a boxed
toaster from the uppermost shelf—you'd maneuver the box
free with your fingertips or a ruler and then you'd leap, and as
you landed, lightly, the box would come to rest right-side-up
in your arms.

It's the early fifties, before the low income projects,
named for social reformers and muckrakers of the turn
of the century—Jacob Riis, Lillian Wald—that fill the one block
from the H & D Housewares Company to the East River,
have become less inhabitable than the decayed tenements
above and alongside the store, years before the junkies
and young thugs became so cocky and unpredictable that
you, always on good terms with an earlier generation of thieves
and hustlers (though you never handled their stolen
goods), even you began to close early, no longer able to
rely on your good name and the heavy stick—was it an
ax handle?—that you kept below the cash register, embarking,
though you had no way of knowing it at the time, on the
grinding march towards your unwilling sale of the store

in 1963, fifteen years after you'd scraped together enough
money and experience to open your own business with
Mr. Davidson, who had less experience and more money, in a
partnership sealed by a handshake after only two conversations.

That handshake was a world and seven years away
from your first job in Brooklyn after you emigrated from
Winnipeg to New York City in 1941. Mother told me the story,
and I can imagine you clearly from the pictures from those
days, lean and handsome, with curly brown hair, in a white
apron, working for Uncle Yossel's sister, Surka, in her grocery.
I can see you watching, pale blue eyes alert, as you hauled
milk crates from the basement, pretending not to notice as she
routinely cheated her customers by, for instance, writing a
one before a forty-nine cent sale on the weekly tab she
was kind enough to keep for her poorest customers in that last
summer of the great depression.

I remember your words, "That Davidson. Never sick
a day in his life. And when his stomach starts acting up,
he makes jokes: 'Your ulcer is lonely, Harry,' he liked to say,
'so my belly decided to keep it company' He used to take
a shot of whiskey, first once, then two, even three times a day."
He always told you how good he felt afterwards, how he
was "burning" the sickness away.

"Poor Davidson! 'Harry,' he'd say, 'Harry, you know
why you're sick all the time? It's on account of you're
always rushing off to doctors. It's been a good ten years since
I seen one, and that was the time I cut my arm on that pane
of glass. Fourteen stitches, and I was back to work the next
day." You always smiled and shook your head at the number,
fourteen, as you are doing right now. And when Davidson
finally gave in to you and mother and his wife, Sylvia, and went
to the doctor, his insides were so riddled with cancer that he
was gone in six weeks. I've always associated Davidson's death
with Uncle Yossel's comment, after he, another supremely
healthy man, also got nailed by cancer. "S'hot mir g'catched,"
it caught me, he said.

It took more than twenty years, but finally it caught
you too, though in your case it was a stroke, not cancer.
I don't know much about death or cancer, and I guess your
heart attacks should have made it less of a shock, but here
we sit, you, in your wheel chair, the soul of your language
shattered to atoms by the stroke, I, gazing at you,
talking and thinking to you about the past, and I have no
certainty at all that my words are getting through any
better than my thoughts, not knowing whether that smile
and nod a few moments ago merely mirrored my gesture or
the tone of my voice or were an acknowledgment of
the word, "fourteen." And as I sink in to this naugehyde
hospital chair, it's easy for me to feel the dampness and
roughness of those painted railings squeeze through my shorts
and chill my darkly tanned thighs as I adjust my legs around
the rail and I look down and I'm wearing yellow shorts
and polished brown shoes with white socks sliding down into
them, and I couldn't have been any more than eight.
    I look up and out towards the breakers, and you're
getting smaller, briskly walking in a gray boxer bathing
suit, a yellow towel around your shoulders, your very white
skin glowing in the moonlight. Now you're bending,
unbuckling your sandals, folding the towel neatly on top of
them, and carefully topping the heap with your glasses.
The sand has lost its brown tincture, the Atlantic Ocean
is black, and the foam from the breaking waves glints more
brightly than your skin. Now the sound reaches me across the
years and I watch you enter the water, walk out till the
bottom of your bathing suit gets wet, and you take a double
handful of water in your cupped hands and slosh it against
your face. I don't know whether I saw you clearly that
time from the boardwalk or that I've seen you enter the water
so many times that way that my mind is feeling in the details.
But I can see the slight white splash as you dive in and I
can make out your hands and forearms as they cut through
the water, though as you swim out, far out, way over

your head, I gradually lose sight of you, and I start playing my
nightly game of guessing which sudden splash of white in
the distance is you, and it always scares me a little as I
try to trace your path, and my imagination always betrays me
because I'm always surprised by your location later when
I catch clear sight of you emerging from the water. Sometimes
it's so dark by then that I'm still looking out at the Atlantic
when I hear you walking through the sand, suddenly just a few
strides from the wooden staircase that rises from the beach
to the boardwalk. You're always full of joy and drops of water.
"There's nothing like it. Nothing in the whole world," you
say, only partly to me.

June 1977

I remember, it was during the first week after you
were stricken that you began to play with the fingers of your
right hand. You lifted first the small finger, then the ring
finger, then the middle finger, one by one, the hand hanging
palm downward, hooklike in its sling, and you watched
with what seemed like detached curiosity, as each finger in
its turn, then your hand, sprang back downward to its lifeless
dangling, and you continued this action for about fifteen
minutes, sometimes plucking one finger three or four
times, sometimes holding the hand or finger still for a few
seconds before letting it drop. Then you looked up at me and
you sagged as if an enormous sadness had come over you.

It was that afternoon that you cooperated for the first
time with the physical therapist, and those brief bursts of
bitterly sarcastic laughter which you had fired at mother and
me vanished for good, along with your attempts to tear the
covers from your bed, the IV tube from your arm, the feeding
tube from your mouth, and the condom catheter from
your penis. Also gone were your terrible cries of "ber BELL ber
BELL ber BELL ber BELL," which I heard as "I'm well, I'm well,
I'm well, why am I tied up like this?" Don't get me wrong.
I'm not saying that you have become sanguine about

your condition. You still, on occasion, shake your fist at me
or clench my forearm in your good left hand in anger or
despair and far too often weep small tears with a look of bitter
and sad puzzlement in your eyes.

Summer 1947

Among my earliest memories are Sundays at the
beach, you all wrapped up in towels, a plaid cotton bathrobe,
and a white canvas hat, a few patches of your skin
showing, on a green shaded beach chair with white fringes.
My legs and arms were chubby (imagine!) and dark,
dark brown from all those long summer days on the beach.
At the center of all those Sundays was you taking me "out for
a swim." Mother used to sit on her beach chair all day,
read, feed all of us, talk to her friends, knit, and periodically
"take a dip" with "the girls." These dips consisted of going
into the water, hunkering down a little, knees bent, back
to the waves, and letting the splash and spray of the
ocean slide or splatter up her back to her shoulders. She
adored the ocean breezes, the salt air, the salt water,
but I don't recall ever seeing her face in the water. She never
swam, as she never danced.

As for you, I've never seen anyone swim as you did.
Your head and the top of your shoulders always above
the water as you swam, your white arms would come out,
then quickly slice side-armed into the water, leaving
barely a ripple as they cut through. It looked so neat and
effortless I wouldn't have known the power of your stroke if
I hadn't ridden on your back, my hands holding your
collar bones, sometimes holding on to your neck for dear life
as you pulled us toward the deep water. Sometimes it
would be the pause and slide, pause and slide of the breast
stroke which I knew you could do forever, or you would cradle
me in front of you as you side-stroked along, or your arms
would envelop me in what seemed to be my own private little
pool in the middle of the Atlantic. I loved how you swam.

I loved swimming with you, and, for years, before anyone
taught me the ins and outs of the crawl, I tried in my bungling
way to teach myself your stroke. But out there, alone with
you in the Atlantic Ocean, I felt no more than a trace,
a tremor, of the fear I later felt when swimming on the top
of very deep water, no, time and time again, I would be so
caught up, so mastered by your power and the tides, that
I wouldn't notice until we were far out, way past the end of
the rotting wooden jetties, that we were alone out there,
that the umbrellas on the shore were tiny splotches of color,
and that the nearest swimmers shone in the distance like
tarnished dimes between us and the beach.

After Midnight

I could have died tonight. The left front wheel
rattled sharply, then rolled from my car: I hadn't
tightened the lugs after changing the spare.
The child in me who thinks he'll bring his mother joy
died a little more. I've been awake

too long. On my way to bed, I slipped
inside Hedya's open door, delicately turned
the knob and pushed Gabi's door open,
then Rebecca's, pausing over
two beds and a crib. I hovered at each station
as each emerged from her darkness into
a barely discernible shape at the far
end of my perception. The familiar
breathing—Hedya's easy on her back, Gabi's
faint growling under the covers
on her side, the baby laboring on her belly,
bottom-up—drew me in, strained my eyes
that yearned to draw them into light. I almost feel

my pupils widening. They
comfort me. I let myself be bathed
in my solicitude. I use my daughters—
indulgently. If I'm here at all
to them, I am some scary or familiar
presence, lurking just out of sight
in the deepest crannies of their dreams,
some household god or totem who at least
believes he would kill or die
to keep them from harm.

To My Wife

Some times
when we grab an hour of love
luxuriously in the late afternoon,
the growly baby snoring in the next room,
her sisters at the mall,
I feel as if I'm robbing the gods, who have,
some say, all the time in the world.

Be with Me

"Be with me, Dad!" you pipe from your bed
as I turn out the light four hours past your bedtime,
that Dad, as always, cracking me up, Joy-Bringer,
and I lay down on my back, my head at the foot
of the bed, your legs between my arms and my side.
Your hands find my hand. Your fingers turn, poke, slap,
and clap quietly with my hand, then you breathe in,
sigh,
and fold them together on your belly. Soon
they're at my hand again, then back on your belly.
I place my hand on yours as lightly as I can.
They settle down, a tiny trembling tapping
my palm like a ladybug's wings or a
birdsong heard after the sound has faded.

Your breathing is regular now, a hint of a snuffle
in your nose: it's time to leave. Slowly I lift
my hand and place it on the sheet. Frantic,
your fingers flutter along my knuckles and wrist,
then leap to their place of rest. My hand
follows: again the trembling and my mind
returns from unheard songs and ladybugs
to where it, too, belongs.

The Spell: To My Wife from Land's End

Will he put up with the constant muddle and squalor which small children bring?
—Peter Abelard, *Historia calamitatum*

Three loads of damp laundry draped on two wood
frame clothes dryers clog the kitchen, so you have walked
from the table in the dining room, through the living room,
past Rebecca's door, and, opening Gabi's a crack,
you have crossed through Hedya's cave to read to me—
dreaming on our bed, writing—passages about
the teachers, therapists, and healers you've been teaching.
At the table, again, you are being pulled back here now
by these words I am writing, I realize,
only to call you, to draw you once more across
the treacherous landscape between us. Five
minutes of this incantation, and you're here. Of course,
in twenty seconds you're gone again, and now I'm
far too awake to cast the spell a second time.

Mother's Night

Again, Linda, we've come back to Hedya,
Rebecca, tears, and fury. After a while
weeping quietly, Rebecca will say,
"Daddy I usually cross my fingers
when you and Mommy leave and Hedi's baby-sitting,
but when she makes faces at me and is mean to me,
I just uncross my fingers
because I know it will be bad
and turn out to be a bad night."

After a while you'll say to her,
"I don't think one of you is good and one
of you is bad," and before long
you'll be into your "Rockedy Rockedy Raggedy Ann,"
your "La La Looo," and the Sh'ma,
and as your lullaby voice rises sweetly,
I will be stumbling into my old love for you
from the first time ever I heard you sing . . .

but the next thing I know
I'm sitting in the dining room
and you're talking to Hedya in the bathroom
so softly I can't make out your words,
trying to take her down
to the source of her sorrow—
"And I hate myself
when she gets me to hate her so much"
is what I'm sure I hear her blurt, gasping,
between bursts of sobs to you, sitting in the tub,
naked, as you were sitting, it must have been
five years ago, only
it's not Hedya who's wailing, it's Gabi,
frustrated in her tears and her fury over hatred and Hedya.
And the words, The Words, are the same. And it's

Mother Daughter Mother Daughter Mother Daughter
Mother Daughter and I've stepped off the edge

of this good planet, giddy
dizzy adrift
somewhere someone's
clumsy arms are flailing vaguely . . .

and *this* time it's your voice I grab hold of,
Linda, crooning the end of the Sh'ma
to Rebecca, and I yank myself back by *this* love,
to *these* words and *this* dining table, writing
in the unsteady light of the kitchen fixture around midnight,
and Gabi's key has found the front door lock
and Hedya has clicked the toaster oven on.
"Why are you up, Bernie?" she's saying sweetly.
"Why don't you put more light on?"

Coming and Going

The sun, the sea a green transparency, the sky,
Rebecca, Gabi, Hedya gone away
to Palmer and Toronto, you and I
on our own, an event! to be savored,
crushed between palate and tongue like the ripe
blackberries we'll pick next month; you and I:
the beach, of all places, Sunday morning,
of all times, though it's Falmouth, not Herzliya,
the Buzzard's Bay chop, not the billowy
Mediterranean waves, and not to be
stepped on, it's broken shells and stones, not zefet.
It's where we've come long married, where you sit,
reading, and I stand, slowly rubbing lotion into
my grizzled cheeks. It's not where we met
years back, you walking up in blue bikini, I
alone on a small towel. But it is now:
"Daddy, come in, please, come in, Daddy, now,"
an eight-year-old daughter jumping a dance to her beat,
hollering to her skinny blond father the lie that
"The water's warm, please, please, Daddy, oh, please, now."
Or is it Gabi or Hedi or Becca
thirteen years ago or five or seventeen:
"Now, oh, now," only this time I'm the Distracted
Daddy (with a thick black beard) taking his time
with a daughter, less time by far, it's true,
than this skinny guy and you . . . I turn, and you're
smiling too, but behind you the sun has flamed
a form in the sand . . . plastic looking seaweed?
No. It *is* plastic, a horse, upside down
in the sand the length of my palm, a toy
I would play with for hours, sculpting my bedspread
into mesas and canyons in the daytime,
under the covers in secret caverns at night,
spinning elaborate adventures
of cowboys and Indians, riding, riding

on the beach, too, the same gray horse, the same
embroidered saddle, the same tail undulated
in the wind when I was an eight-year-old
tugging at my father's plaid cotton robe, saying, "Daddy,
oh, now, now, please," to my white-skinned father
at last rising from his beach chair and slowly asking
his wife, deadpan. "What do you think, Bella,
I should take him for a swim?"

I could tell you that the horse must have come
tumbling from Rockaway Beach
to the Cape through the sand and the years,
avoiding the comforts of the sun and the rain
and falling snow, winding its way underground
along the coast without sound,
just so I would write, on the inside cover
of *The Brothers K* a love poem for once
in your presence, that contains a toy
I decide to leave here, a shadow
to be lost forever, unless
recaptured in the sand tomorrow
by some eight-year-old I'll never see, but who,
though no one even will dream it at the time,
will remember the moment for the rest of his life.

In These Eternities
a Great Sadness Lingers

There you and I swam and nodded off,
and the baby, guarded by his mother,
slept erect in the back harness, the soft
blue foreign legionnaire's hat
protecting his neck from the late July sun
as his five-year-old sister and her pal
negotiated boulders and stones and covertly
threw quick glances back at us, their
body-length towel capes flapping in the soft wind
that was reaching all the way around to us
from the Sound.

There, one day later, three mothers, daring,
and double daring, venture around our little cape
to the next cove where they swim in their nakedness
out of sight of *our* two daughters, older,
fully seventeen and twenty-five, stretched out
on their towels, tanning languorously
and laughing in complicitous amusement
at the three mothers, and at me, too,
alone with them in our cove, as I, sedulous,
protect this approach to the mothers' adventure
as I had guarded one of those mothers
in the birthing room seventeen years back,
when one of those daughters
made her stark entrance into this world.

There, then, the salt air, salt lips, the white salt streaks
scratched along my tanning skin fling me
down the sand and sea stained years back
to a decade of summers—one long summer day—
those lunches of tuna sandwiches on rye, ambrosial
peaches, and apricots, the luscious plums, those slow

evenings of lime rickeys and vanilla custards,
those slower days of sand castles, catching crabs,
and riding the waves, endlessly,
in an eternity that is futile to contemplate
in the forty years that have followed,

as my father, gone fifteen years this Elul, stands there
in the low surf, his white skin glowing just after sunset,
and splashes handfuls of saltwater into his face
and plunges neatly under the next breaker,
and the other amused daughter crawls on all fours
at the edge of another sea, scurrying along,
an ocean, a continent, and a quarter century away,
nine months old and naked there
in her brimmed white sun bonnet with red polka dots,
which I can see, my love, only in your story: she,
scuttling along, knocked over by wavelets rolling back
on all fours, laughing and crawling, tumbling and laughing,
as I keep tumbling, back
into these, the only eternities
I know, only I'm not laughing.

Rebecca's Eighteen

Night swallows fall light.
Yellow, red, wind-blown, they surge:
"Go, kick the leaves, now!"

It Was Either

It was either pitch them or do what I did
tonight, so I ate the two plums you had chosen
carefully which were already falling apart,
purple skin wrinkling up, flesh exposed—
and, yes, they exploded whole,
deliciously in my mouth, both gulped
in less than a minute
and, yes, I have to say that I did
wash all the others and I did place
the two ripest and the sweetest (I have no doubt)
on top of the other six in a glass bowl for you
carefully, which is all I have to say tonight,
my love.

three:

paint her

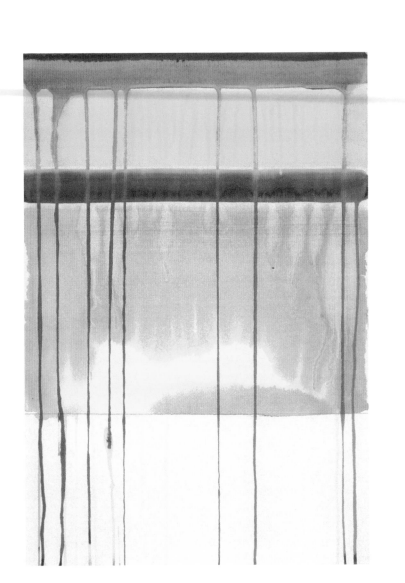

Magic

The residue of stone age imagination
that placed the elephant with the heart,
stags with twisted antlers,
fighting crescent horned ibexes, spear pierced
and bellowing bison, honeybees,
generations of game
on the walls of the hunters' caves
at Lascaux, Altamira,
Le Roc de Sers, and Montespan,
locks the tan macramé wall hanging
to the wall by my desk:
a present knotted for me
by the fingers of someone I'll never
see again and never forget,
who years before
knotted my blue key chain
so worn now it no longer brings her to mind
though she lives in the hanging
on the wall by the window
opposite my eyes as I work at this desk
where once worked a poet
who knew the knots of the nets of being
that no sword cuts.

The Conversion of Saint Paul

A horse's ass
viewed from the rear, off white,
poised with its dark rider

in a rough and narrow mountain pass
packed with laden soldiers and tattered camp followers,
spears, horses, a whole army on the move

from the Holy Land to Damascus
is what Breughel throws at our first glance
at his painting.

Deep in the crowd, small
and blue, puffed sleeves, wispy brown hair,
a little to the right and above

the exact center of the painting, sprawls Paul,
just fallen, next to his horse,
brought to its knees. Only

the barely discernible men in the small clearing
around Paul, faces and arms flung upwards
toward the yellow light,

only the few pale rays
near the highest branches of the cedars that tower
above the huge and

craggy gorge, only
the distant sea and sky at the horizon shining
ultramarine blue and white

intimate that there is
miracle here not passing dream
and how it matters.

Aura

(for Linda)

"Let me tell you: when I'd look at those landscapes
by Leonardo and Breughel reproduced in art books,
my eyes having rested only on the greens
and darks and grays of Massachusetts
and Pennsylvania, Colorado and Israel,
somehow there was always something
about those landscapes I loved that I couldn't
get hold of—I just wasn't convinced the old masters
painted what they saw—it must have been fantasy, I thought,

"and now as I walk the Rhone Valley at Leuk,
looking uphill at vineyards, and downhill, looking
at the faces of rocks or at arrays of small waterfalls
erupting from springs of primordial coldness,
looking across at the mountain wooded like stubble
at its crest or at the strangely milky river
that opens my eyes to the great valley
opening westward toward Geneva—

"suddenly, it is that landscape: the old masters
painted what they saw or the forms they saw
in what they saw in this new landscape
that astounds me with the fierceness of my oldest memories:

"and whether I gaze at the landscape or gaze
at the paintings, all that I take in leans in on me
and implicates me in the ground, the stance,
the gestures of those painters who also gazed
and also squinted as their eyes moved from the world
to the canvas, from the canvas to the world
as they worked in every single shade of green
under the good sun."

Paint Her

Paint her, I said, taken once again
as if for the first time, by that look
on that face—it must have been three years ago—
caught in the eight-and-a-half-by-eleven
xerox of a black-and-white close-up
on the fridge: at fifteen, a tinge of sadness
and unspeakable fragility that starts
to vibrate, to appear, and to recede
around her eyes and along the corners
of her mouth as my eyes
linger—a look not so different

from the face in the photo of the little girl
in the blue print dress. She was three then.
Who would have thought a little girl
could have so many feelings in her? Then,
too, a painful, an even more delicate
oscillation of emotion as a gaze
lingers, the look

entirely different, too, each image
only itself—brand-new, eternal—creating
and recreating my life and your life
as you try to contain the heart's indescribable fugue
that mingles image and memory with our living daughter
who'll be home from school any second and the futility
of trying to get it all down in paint, its beauty.

Color

(for Stanley Moss)

. . . which so incorruptibly reduced a reality to its color
content that that reality resumed a new existence
in a beyond of color without any previous memories.
        —Rainier Maria Rilke, *Letters on Cézanne*

In the Last Room of the MOMA retrospective,
a cul de sac, the grays and blacks
of the final compositions press
down heavily: unbearable, the black above,
the gray below, the straight edge between
give back nothing, nor do they invite long, slow
contemplation (like the others). No, they,
no, no, they say, no. Firmly. Still. I flit
from one large canvas to another. No. There are simply
too many to handle. Outnumbered, I retreat,
backing out through the entrance to that terminus,

into Color. My eyes fill, my breath,
too, deeply, as I turn away and pan the Next-to-Last Room,
pausing, glancing. I turn again and will
my way back across the threshold
of the Last Room through the wide proscenium
into anxiety (or is it tragedy?). Then out, then in
for one more try, until, routed, I plop down
in the Next-to-Last Room on a bench
that happens to face a late painting,
dark gray above dark gray on maroon,
and I relax, gazing into the alluring
boundary where color embraces—no,
does not embrace—color, as the squarish masses
above and below open, hover, and deepen, this time
inviting, not contemplation, but rapture, even as the whole
vast surface precludes in its abstraction a glimmer

of certainty, the merest glint of one meaning, or
several, and I hear the faint rush of
air through my nostrils and I notice my breathing has evened,
and in this thing I am feeling I know all there is
and poor Rothko's terrible role: The First Artist of Color:
this confluence of mind, eye and hand precisely
like those paintings of game performed
on the walls of the sacred galleries
at the wombs of the hunters' caves at Lascaux
and Altamira, but with this difference: as long as there
is drawing on the walls of the caves, there is game
in the forest; *as long as there is color on these paintings,
there is color in the world,* and perhaps in the end
it is too much, a burden heavier than the sky,
to keep color in the world. I shake my head, and, as I do,
I feel my neck muscles knot up and I turn slowly
for a last look through the severe threshold
into the Last Room. Let's go, I tell myself.
I do not move.

A Fork

She is your life,
the life you fear, the life
you desire, your own private
temptation, sitting right there on the sidewalk
a yard from the curb
on Madison Avenue in the seventies,
grasping two shopping bags full of
god knows what, a red sheen
on her polished face, in kerchief, khaki raincoat,
thick gray sweater this late spring day promising summer,
your urge is
to join her on the sidewalk, to leave
us and the galleries here and in Chelsea
and SoHo, to leave your desire
for the galleries and your first career
on track at last after a twenty-five year
digression that, as you say,
is your life
as human being, woman,
wife, mother, wife, again, mother, again:
as god-wrestler: at this moment an attraction
almost irresistible is drawing you
to join her there on the sidewalk
or, to be reasonable about it, to take her home
with us, to feed her, to see her as someone
sitting down to supper with all of us
routinely: to hear her story.

The Florence Pietà

In the reflecting surface
of the finished marble that extends
from twisted foot and ravaged leg
to chest, Michelangelo caught the split second
when immortality—which I imagine
rising slowly from the ground upward
as the man Jesus is dying in his mother's lap—
reached the region of his heart,
his turned face and eyes still mortal
and anguished, like Mary's,
and, brooding above them,
the bearded and hooded Nicodemus,
a self-portrait of the anguished, aging sculptor
who had smashed the work after eight years
of labor: the rough unfinish of the marble
in the upper regions of the sculpture
the dead giveaway, the quotation from Psalms,
"My God . . . forsaken me,"
still on his lips, an instant
or eternity
before it is finished.

Proxy

Another new terrain for us at sixty-four and sixty-six,
my love: these long gray corridors at 6:00 a.m.,
the wide green stripe halfway up the wall leading
to Surgical Waiting. You're here
to have your knee replaced.

Before we part, you to pre-op, I to
wait, you turn in the proxy form.

Routine, I try to think. Not so routine, that form last night,
to you or me, to Hedi or Becca—you with the oddest of looks
in your eyes—and it isn't long before
suddenly I barely can breathe, anxiety thickening my chest
just as the surgery begins its second hour
8:30 a.m. this gray drizzly June morning.

I walk outside and in and read and sit and walk and
stand around, but there's no place for me in the world
until one hour later when the surgeon,
looking no more than thirty, appears to say the surgery
"went perfectly"; your leg has returned to its proper form:

straight (the cobalt chrome-capped femur in its proper place
above the titanium-capped tibia), the inner meniscus
of magical plastic cushioning
the alloy caps and my morning blues,

minutes before Hedi and Becca arrive and I begin to breathe
and we begin to wait together. I do not tell our daughters
what I'd waded through that second hour of surgery
or the number of times "proxy proxy proxy"
screeched in my mind that morning,
the word reduced to pure sound,
or the chorus of some pack of harpies,
drilling, deeply, heard in a shadowy place
of concern, true, but something else, too,
ruled by the thought of life without you.

"Wait!" I tried to tell myself. "This surgery is routine.
Your fears are wacky. The surgeon's a master. There is
nothing to be ashamed about."
But, no I realized, it was never the surgery—
there is something about general anesthesia
that transformed me into someone capable of
savoring the taste and sound of mourning
that was staining my lips and ears—

that harpy scream that filled my morning
was only, I now knew, a subterfuge, for in its place,
my eyes closed–my ears becoming eyes—I heard the keening
of an irregular crowd of black-cloaked women

and I was among them!— "Poor me"
were the words coming to form
out of nowhere and then the shame

of thinking of myself at such a moment
in that berserk vision of a black cloud of crying women
in a corridor leading to a pale room,
the mirror of Surgical Waiting,
reserved, I realized, for the survivors
of surgeries gone awry.

Back to myself, I came face to face
with the fear and the grief, of course, and the shame,
too, the self-pity that was opening wide
at the thought of waking one morning

alone. My God! It hadn't crossed my mind
that surgery would open such places.
But you knew, my love, didn't you? That
was what I saw in your eyes last night as you
waited for us to sign that form.

four:

two or three things

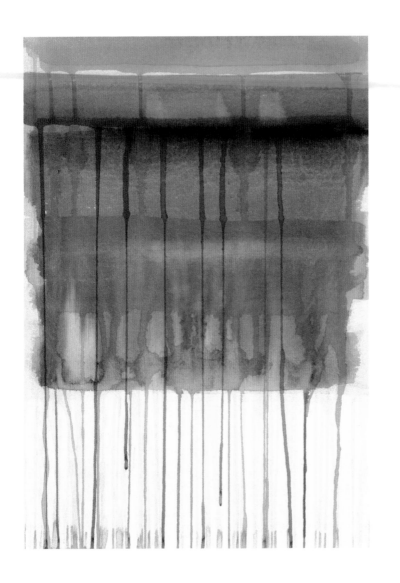

Valentine 1994

What I've learned from nearly fifty years
is hard to say,

Calvin having disappeared
two raging snowstorms and five days ago
and I surprised to find myself peering
out and down from our third floor windows
four, five, even six times a night, squinting
as I tried to make out his paw prints
in the unbroken white sheen of the snow,
not realizing how intently I'd been listening, too,
until his faint meow reached me, half asleep,
last night, in our bed, around midnight;

and our dear pal Becky pregnant at last, yes,
and buffeted all day long, week after week,
by furious hurricanes of morning sickness;

and Robert still
my oldest friend,
though he has drifted away
these last six years
—suddenly the news:
ravaged by cancer
he's dying.

There's nothing here that you don't know,
but I'm thinking how happy we were
when we stopped saying the prayer to be safe
under the sheltering wings of peace
which we had added, during the Gulf War,
to the Friday night blessings at home
before you lit the candles,

and how, the Friday night after the war had ended,
after services, a woman I barely knew had asked,

"How are you?" and I managed to blurt,
"The war is over," before I felt the tears
gathering at the corners of my mouth,
faintly detected the salt between my tongue
and my lips and noticed her shifting vague features,
the near panic in her scurrying eyes, and knew
how odd my words had sounded to her.

We shared happiness that night three years ago
(when I finally reached you
chatting with Bob and Meryl
on the other side of the crowded room)
as we had shared the fear,
thinking of nothing else for days at a time
as the SCUDS seemed to track Gabi's every move
from her home in Tel Aviv to Ramat Aviv and Ra-anana,
from Jerusalem to Be-er Sheva—nothing
could have brought us closer. We
had been married ten and a half years.

Chicken

I have to admit it was a long way
from the night you were seeing wild dogs
along the floor in the short corridor
between your bedroom and the bathroom
and I had to hold you up because we had
no choice but to walk through this dense pack
that yelped and snapped as you pressed your back
against the closet door sidling crablike,
but slowly, inch by inch, your eyes fixed downward,
your feet oddly contorted, desperate not to touch
the ground, my right arm holding you firmly
against my side as your left fist clenched
and unclenched my pants and the fingers
of your right hand flickered for balance in the air.

Today it was only supper and the way
you were eating the pulka, as you used to call it,
the drumstick, of the boiled chicken. I'd never seen
you eat this way before, holding it in your hand,
your mouth really working it over,
sucking it clean, putting the whole top of the bone in
your mouth to get at every last morsel,
and it coming to me at once
that this must be exactly how you did it,
mother, at your father's table in Uman
eighty-five years ago.

Ein Bokek

(for Gabi and Dani)

When we descended in the shaking and pitching jeep,
gears grinding, wheels whirring when they caught
pebbles and air, we thought we would tumble, all of us,
head over heels, crashing to the bottom, the newlyweds,
the sisters of the bride, the father of the bride
and his lover, the mother and her husband, all of us
dog tired, having grabbed a couple of hours of sleep
on carpets in an enormous Bedouin tent somewhere
in the Judean Wilderness after the evening
wedding ceremony there under a chupah made of a
talit that flapped so hard on its poles in the night wind
that the rabbi wrapped it around the shoulders of the
bride and groom and declared "an old tradition" under
the black and star-packed sky; at the wheel, when we
descended, the groom, who knows this rough and
desolate landscape, is amused at all our clinging to
each other and hollering:
all of us and everything, the jeep,
our skin and clothes, mustaches and eyebrows, were
ghosts, coated with the fine talc of the desert sand.
We were so dry when we hit bottom, we didn't hesitate,
we plunged fully clothed into the bitter waters
of the spring that gives Ein Bokek its name:
the Spring of Desolation, not even thinking our clothes
would dry in minutes in the sun drenched Dead Sea air.
We didn't drink the water: laughing and splashing,
we drank everything in at the mouth of the spring,
the newlyweds, the family, the water: so wet, so clear!

Letter from Israel (March 3, 2001)

Adam was created alone to teach us that anyone
who destroys one life is considered by the Torah as
if he had destroyed the whole world and anyone
who saves one life is considered by the Torah as if
he had saved the whole world.
                    —Babylonian Talmud: Sanhedrin 37a

The big news from Israel is that a week ago
Thursday Lyla—not quite two, remember—
let Linda and me, her "Dida" and "Papa,"
pick her up from gan for the first time
without Gabi or Dani; that every night
on the counter by the tub she does her "bath dance"
in front of a huge mirror, naked
except for the "hat" made of a shirt
pulled inside out at the top of her head,
long-sleeved, because she must
have her long ears to swing all around her
as she dances; that Dani spent all day yesterday
preparing a Shabbat birthday feast for Linda,
of eggplant appetizers, a chicken
and Calamata olive stew, and the densest of cheesecakes
with lychees thrown in; that I walked past the corner
of Montefiore and Allenby ten times
last month, six times alone (four times
in two hours Tuesday because I'd grabbed
a big tan envelope from the kitchen table
on the way out and only discovered at the visa office
that the envelope was full of poems,
not passport and photos and documents)
and twice more with Linda
and twice more with Linda and Gabi
and Lyla—our only desires
were to wrestle with bureaucrats,
buy housewares for our place,

buy shoes for Lyla; that I wouldn't
be telling you all this except that the man
from Hamas who blew up the taxi at the Mei Ami junction
on Thursday, murdering Claude Knafu of Tiberias
and injuring nine more, planted a bomb
at a shwarma place, Brothers', at the corner
of Montefiore and Allenby some time
Tuesday evening: a bomb spotted by the owner,
set off by sappers, wrecking the shop,
hurting no one at all; that I almost forgot to tell you
that Lyla says "Mommy carry you!"
when she wants Gabi to pick her up, that she says
"ani rotzah la'aloat al ha yellow one"
about her favorite swing in the little park
around the corner; that, somehow, mysteriously,
she says "hair" and "ear" with an Israeli resh;
that on the way to Tsfat with Larry and Karen
on Sunday, we stopped for fresh figs at the roadside stand
at the Mei Ami junction; and that
if there are any eyes in the world brighter
than Lyla's I haven't seen them.

So There It Is

So there it is: the siren. It's 10 am. The three of us
stand up around the table in the small dinette—
for some reason we all face the window
and the birds are chirping their heads off.
In my mind are my father's losses: sister, big brother,
his wife, his two sons—and the story my mother told me
just last year very carefully, shaking off for a moment
the slowly rising flood of confusion and timelessness
that more and more is her life these days:
that when they visited Yad Vashem in '77,
one month before his final stroke, my father had fainted,
having discerned his brother among the open sea of faces
there. And in my mind, it's yitgadal v'yitkadash
for Motek and Rina and the wife and sons
whose names I don't know (and for my father, too) and
the next thing I know it's my first
Yom Ha-Shoah in Israel nine years back
on a highway in the middle of the Negev at 10 am,
the few cars to be seen in the wide and flat terrain
pulled over to the side under a big sky, and by each of them
one or two figures standing silent and now,
breaking into and penetrating the drone of the siren
is the silly musical phrase calliope-like
they use instead of a bell to mark the end of each class
in the school across the way and one minute
has elapsed and before I know it
the siren is rising in pitch and two minutes are gone
and there is silence for a beat,

and for that second minute, I realize,
there were neither birds nor inner words nor memory
nor breath, for one entire minute, all there was
was the sound of the siren and that was all there was.

Neighbors

There's no such thing as was only is.
If was existed there'd be no grief or sorrow.

At ease in the back yard, late afternoon, under the trellis,
sipping coffee and the sweet smell of spring:
at once, a scraping sound, nearby:
aged it was and human in terrible half-mad complaint.
Next door, behind the high shrub.
In bursts the scratching rises in pitch,
the language—and it is a language—Hebrew? Yiddish?
German? Polish? Hungarian?—a pure sound of
unimaginable . . . grief? sadness?—

And another voice there, all along,
male, quiet, patient, not condescending,
I noted—barely discernible, a continuo
all around the bursts, and silent I looked at Dani
at the far end of the rough-hewn picnic table on the patio,
and he: "Oh, it comes over her
late in the afternoon,
often . . . a survivor."

It was Faulkner who said, I recalled,
"There's no such thing as was, only is."
When Dani sees her outside, she's not this way,
he said. "A little strange, perhaps,
but nothing this extreme." So when I was caught,
a week later, hemmed in by high shrubs on the narrow path
near our front door, late in the afternoon
of Yom Hashoah, by the hectic brown eyes
of a tall woman with a deeply wrinkled face
and a fine old-fashioned black
print dress and bedroom slippers
torn through, the padding bursting out,

I knew it was she and thought back
to Dani and me sitting there quietly
for a beat or two. It was something
to be expected, those late afternoon sounds,
to grow used to.

Art, Vienna

From the first her second language was art.
She wasn't more than four, I recall, when words
failed her once as she tried to describe a dance-
like move by our cat, Calvin. She turned on the light,
grabbed a sheet of paper, and drew a perfect
string of images, which I can see, as I drift back to Vienna,

where she and you and I sat in the very worst seats in the Vienna
State Opera thirty years later. Yes, there are other arts
besides the visual, we agreed, wowed by the near-perfect
performance of *Don Carlo*. This time, no loss of words
for her or you or me: we were a trio of delight,
our bubbling sounds and movements a silly dance

of life along streets that for a thousand years delighted in a dance
of death for such as we, but times have changed in charming
    Vienna.
Imagine! We stood deeply underground and alive in the
    well-lighted
ruins of the ancient synagogue. Reading there it hit me, the art
of murder, no, the art of extermination—let's not mince words—
had been practiced here for centuries before it was perfected.

Who knew? Between the first Crusade and the Holocaust—it's
    too perfect—
there was another little holocaust—Duke Albert's—one more dance
of death, a 1421 bonus, ravaging synagogue and every Jew, but
    word
has not yet reached the texts at tourist traps where the supreme
    Viennese
confection, the amnesia-torte, rules the roost, the pinnacle of
    household art
that scurries in the undergrowth afraid of light.

Now, every summer, she fashions images there from lowly
      objects and light,
transforming lucent plastic forms and pastel bags into perfectly
glowing inner landscapes and dreamlike cities. Is this rare art—
that mingles foul objects and transience in a luminous dance—
so imaginative and so sublime that somehow hard Vienna
itself can be transformed as well, in a realm too deep for words,

that resists the despairing heft of the most terrible words
of all? Holocaust . . . Extermination . . . Can a single light-
steeped imagination change the past of that city, Vienna,
which has accomplished a denial, refraction or indifference as
      perfect
as the memory accomplished by others? Memory, denial, Dancer
      dance . . .
Victim, bystander. Does art have limits? I want to know. If limits,
      is it art?

Or is it best for now, my love, to forgo art and revel in how small
      words
or acts of gratitude, respect, and courage can raise a dance of
      light
in the perfect blue eyes of our dear, dear daughter, there in old
      Vienna?

"A Dumb Blankness, Full of Meaning" (May 10, 2001)

Sometimes I sing of moments when there is no time.
Sometimes time is all there is, and the after that is always
here can grasp us by the throat. Here.
Now. Two teenage boys skipping school
to scout around outside their village in the ravine
they think of as their back yard, looking, some said,
for a perfect spot for tonight's bonfire, captured,
and there is a kind of obscenity in writing down
right here right now what happened
(the parents thinking all the while they had crossed
the Green Line to a protest in Jerusalem.)
And all I want to know is what happened:
that they were living there and not elsewhere;
that they, perhaps egging each other on, happened
to play hooky today to some new or old adventure,
that had gotten them to that precise place
at that exact time; that the killers were living there,
so full of wickedness or hatred, righteousness or grief
that they were lurking, or were strangers who just
happened to be there at that place at that moment;
that the boys were stoned to death in a cave,
the killers taking their time with their decision
as they hefted and hurled each stone; that one of them,
at least, dipped his hand in their blood and smeared the walls?

Is there any meaning here? Or is this, no more
or less than the most important thing of all
to so many, simply no more or less than a time
and a place of lawlessness, of violence, entirely
too small for any meaning to stick to, unless
it is to stab us from behind with the thought
of a universe whose law is confusion
or affliction, unless it is the dream that even
in a universe so contrived
the laser cries of children where they are
must slice through?

2006, 1995

These, the dog days of July 2006, with Lyla and her Mama,
Gabi, our eldest, here for four weeks from Tel-Aviv,
and our home is packed for five days with your side
of the family, too, Americans all: your two
surviving sisters, Dian and Lucretia; their daughters,
Vickie and Lizzy, with their kids, Kelly, Zach, and Brooke,
plus Kelly's daughters, Olivia and Amelia:

four generations of American names—Paulsons, Smoots,
Cookes, Wards, Benners—each full name bespeaking
fingerprints, that unique zero point two percent
of the helical spring of identity that makes us who we are.

And somehow—as headlines from Lebanon trickle in—
even in the cacophony of thirteen relatives under one roof
and an excessive cascade of proper nouns,

we have not found it difficult to leap back
eleven years: November 4, 1995,
your first opening at the Bromfield Gallery
and the fourteenth birthday of Becca, our
baby: so lovely a celebration it was!

Long unseen friends and family packing the white space,
surprising you again and again and then not:
as each appeared, you'd smilingly catch my eye. "I'd half
expected Gabi to come waltzing in," you might
have thought. This is something worth surviving
for. But Gabi, of course, was home in Tel-Aviv
that bright November day, living through

the latest catastrophe, which, drip by drip,
was transforming many of us 7000 miles away
into a handful of playground children
in on some terrible secret. "Have you spoken to Gabi?"
was shorthand for the second cosmos
suddenly sprung to life in that white space
where, a split second earlier, there had been

just one, compacted of beauty and joy
(truth too, we might have thought)
before the impact of the assassination in Tel-Aviv
had engendered this second invisible world
as the news came in that Gabi had been
in the peace rally in what will be renamed
Rabin Square but had left before
she got the news, as dance music played
and the Children of Israel did not panic,
and in that white space 7000 miles west,

where I was and I was not, there were now some
to whom I had nothing to say and others for whom
there was but a single word, "Gabi:
have you heard from her?" Gabi,
Gabi, in low voices, shadowing forth
immensities packed with meaning or no meaning
at all, an impossible gap yawning: Us, Them,

that has leapt back to life now, eleven years later
as Kelly's Olivia, age four, great-grandchild
of one sister, plays obliviously with the seven-year-old
grandchild, Lyla, of another, at the same time as the three
of us, Gabi, you, and I, are, in truth, invisible

to them, the grand-nieces and grand-nephew,
the sisters and the nieces, in our home.
We will survive and share the small talk—
which may for all we know become family sayings—

as the news from Lebanon and Israel
fixes our thoughts just now
on two children who died in Nazareth,

as Gabi, child and grandchild of survivors, is pondering
the truth that it is possible to leave home for four weeks
and miss a war, and no doubt we'll survive, again,
she'll pack her bags for home, again,
but the children,

the children!

At Dave & Becky's

On the one hand, it's a long Saturday
early afternoon walk through a nourishing
country landscape, so renewable in fertility,
so human in scale, after a breakfast
of Irish Breakfast tea sipped in weighty cups
hand-thrown by Charlotte, who would join us later
for dinner—and toasted challah,
braided and baked
by Becky ("First you need to bathe,"
she'd told us yesterday, after our long
four hours on the road from the city.)
and poppy seed coffee cake, delicious,
dropped off at the door by the wife
of a Luftwaffe glider pilot—
they arrived in the States after the War,
were abandoned by their sponsor, and on his own,
working hard, he taught himself,
became a master carpenter from a book, both
husband and wife something like grandparents
now to Dave's two young daughters, and that Luftwaffe
beginning has begun to taste a little
gritty to Dave these last years.
Which leads me to the talk. Of how we are
buffeted like sparrows on the huge winds
of history, and the destructiveness,
the idolatry of the whole notion
of progress. Of the deaths of fathers,
of fathers' guilts and the Shoah.
Of returning soldiers afflicted
with post-traumatic stress: whether it's
a physical truth, like the aftermath
of Becky's accident, or an ailment more of the mind,

that strikes when communities break up
and meaning slips beyond the grasp

of the imagination. Of blindness
and bee venom, *The Blue Angel*
and *The Scarlet Empress.* Of a woman
who pulled out every bulb from a flower
garden and the two daughters of a broken marriage
now a continent away from their father
and his new wife, as the older
couples talk of the pain and joy
of grown children who leave home and never leave
and the younger couple edges towards
a new family of their own and a perennial garden—
and all the while, time and again, just
a quick breath after some recollected
loss or outrage, someone mutters
something, and extravagant hilarity
erupts in syncopation and binds
us all, old, old friends and new, in the long
lazy August day that, on the other hand,
is timeless.

Two or Three Things

I am plankton.
—Maurice Sendak

I'm thinking of my blistered inner
arms and my fingers ravaged
by poison ivy or maybe it is
oak this fall, on the one
hand, and, on the other, the breaking news
that Lyla has begun to talk to
everyone, adults
included, at her
kindergarten, and how
I wish that this
were the whole of
the news of the day,

in other words,
that we contain
multitudes and make
and remake our
selves time
after time, and yet

we may find ourselves
some luminous Tuesday
morning late
in the summer
in some tall
building in the heart
of the capital of the world
or on some flight
from here to there.

2009 Old Seventy Creek Press Poetry Series

Our Daily Words by Bernard Horn won the 2009 Old Seventy Creek Press Poetry Series Contest Award.

Bernard Horn

Bernard Horn's poems and translations (of Yehuda Amichai's poetry) have appeared in *The New Yorker, The Manhattan Review, The Mississippi Review, Moment Magazine, Outer Bridge, Dark Horse, Red Crow,* and *Mail.* He is the author of *Facing the Fires: Conversations with A. B. Yehoshua,* the only book in English about Israel's pre-eminent novelist, and his articles on the Bible have appeared in *Shofar* and *Essays in Literature.* He was awarded a Fulbright and five fellowships from the National Endowment for the Humanities. A graduate of the Massachusetts Institute of Technology and the University of Connecticut, he is a professor of English at Framingham State College in Massachusetts. He has three married daughters and three grandchildren and lives in Framingham with his wife, artist Linda Klein.

notes

To Comfort the Heart's Core Against Its Small Disasters.
The title is a variation on a line in Wallace Stevens'
"The Credences of Summer."

Mother's Night. "The Sh'ma" is shorthand for
"Hear, Israel, the Lord is our God, the Lord is one,"
the central Jewish prayer.

Coming and Going. "Zefet" is tar. The last lines echo
lines in Wallace Stevens' "Sunday Morning."

In These Eternities a Great Sadness Lingers. "Elul" is
the last summer month of the Hebrew calendar.

Magic. "Nets of being" is a phrase by Charles Olson.

Ein Bokek. "Chupah" is a wedding canopy.
"Talit" is a prayer shawl.

Letter from Israel (March 3, 2001). "Gan" is Hebrew for
garden or kindergarten. "Resh" is the Hebrew guttural R.

So There It Is. "Yitgadal v' yitkadash" are the opening
words of the Kaddish, the Jewish memorial prayer.
"Yom Ha-Shoah" is Holocaust Memorial Day.

"A Dumb Blankness, Full of Meaning" (May 10, 2001).
The title is from "The Whiteness of the Whale"
in *Moby-Dick.*

Made in the USA
Charleston, SC
05 March 2012